small nights gospel

groell

Copyright © gsoell, 2019

All rights reserved. No part of this publication may be reproduced, stored or transmitted in any form or by any means, electronic, mechanical, photocopying, recording, scanning, or otherwise without written permission from the publisher. It is illegal to copy this book, post it to a website, or distribute it by any other means without permission.

First edition

To Nana
Who created the art that matters the most

To Travis
Who helped create me

Table Of Contents

Forgiveness • 3
My Body • 4
Patterns • 5
Queer • 6
Watering Hole • 7
Detox • 8
57% Cacao • 9
Zenith • 10
Fatalistic • 11
My therapist told me • 12
The Foundation • 13
Beast • 14
Silver Emotion • 15
Where is this? • 16
Weighted • 17
Why I Don't Know Spanish • 18
Trans-Lite • 19
Echoes • 20
Everything Moves Too Fast • 21
Earl Grey • 22
Coming Out • 23
Reflection • 24
Epilogue • 25
Sewing • 26
Missing You • 27
Black Cloak • 28
Valhalla • 29
Music • 30
Insectile • 31
Day of the Dead • 32
Not Like Eliot's Wasteland • 33
Anxiety • 34
It's Too Loud • 35
Boundaries • 36

Moments • 37
Wind • 38
Flaws • 39
Spring • 40
New Wave Cholitas • 41
Hypromellose • 42
Years • 43
Unbalanced • 44
Waiting and watching • 45
Identity • 46
Still • 47
While on break at work • 48
Love Letter • 49
After the initial buzz of alcohol • 50
My first • 51
Fuckability • 52
Queen Mab • 54
Misandry • 56
My parents taught me • 57
Twins • 58
Red Balloon • 59
Hex • 60
our matching tattoos, buffalo wings,
that hood store down the street, the color red • 61
Stop. • 62
Pinocchio • 63
Self-Care • 64
I Wrote This On A Brown Paper Bag • 65
Courage • 66
Excerpts • 67
Guillotine • 70
At Last • 71
Solder • 72
November 5th, 2017 • 73
Yellowing • 74

Crone • 75
Don't Worry, Be • 76
Licorice Noose • 77
As I Lay In Bed with My Lover • 78
It All Comes Together • 79
Tonight • 80
Old Hurt in the Bed • 81
Melting Honey • 82
Why Do I Scare You? • 83
Cracked • 84
Why? • 85
Steel Spine • 86
Giants • 88
Dinner • 89
Your Phone • 90
Punch-Drunk • 91
Substitute Teacher • 92
Trust Me • 93
Temporarily • 94
Tornado • 95
Waves • 96
Bully • 97
Erosion • 98
Is This How You Love? • 99
Cyclical • 101
Bitter • 102
Pavlovian • 103
Argument • 104
To my Rivera • 105
Weekend • 106
My Love • 107
Golden One • 108
The Origins of Thursday • 109
Motherfu- • 110
Fill in the Blank • 111

A God, Magic and A Psych Ward • 112
About the Author • 123

Small Nights Gospel
by gsoell

//prologue//
the gospels are often used as proof of salvation, proof of love. this title *Small Nights Gospel* declares this collection as proof. small nights are when the world feels small, you feel small, your life and love and goodness feel small. you are destined for a stymied existence, never growing. stunted. on these nights, hatred and anger and hurt are a full moon beckoning your tide of blood and bone. tomorrow promises another small night.

this collection is proof that these nights hold concentrated magic. there is magic bound in this book, seeped into every word. I am the end result of a lifetime filled with small nights; some of those nights are when I wrote these words.

this collection is proof that small nights mean something. something potent and significant.
it's proof that I am significant. let it be proof that I was here. that you were here. that you and I and every night is indispensable

Forgiveness
My sister asked me to massage her shoulders.
When I began to rub
the muscle never yielded but
grew harder, resisting.
I suppose that's what I've been doing
and maybe if I soaked in hot water
saw an acupuncturist
let hands rub Tiger Balm into the
whorls of preternaturally tight muscle

I would be able to let go.

My Body
I hold the ocean in my hand
the salty blue fluttering in my palms
wrinkling my fingertips
restless restless.
Waiting.

Patterns

I'm upset tonight.
I stay mad by releasing every tragedy from the box at once
not even hope is left.
I stay stupid just because I can.

I'm upset tonight.
I stay mad by clicking on her profile
thinking of your dick in her mouth.
I stay stupid just because I can.

I'm upset tonight.
I stay mad by gorging on cotton candy fantasies
spinning more improbabilities.
I stay stupid just because I can.

Queer
I want to wrap myself in the skin of every woman.
I crave the sticky sweat as bodies meld into one
And I am decimated.

SMALL NIGHTS GOSPEL by gsoell

Watering Hole
The stranger in the movie theater
hissed *shhh* while I was whispering to my sister
during the beginning of the movie.
I apologized and stewed for two hours
ready to make fists fly
teeth knocked to the sticky popcorn strewn floor.
I settled for crunching ice loudly
crystal shards digging into my tongue
the receded gums on the right side of my mouth screaming
white hot.

Animal rage goaded me into talking louder and longer
hoping the stranger would give me a reason to leave
claw marks down the side of their face
red wet jewels glimmering on my razor tipped fingers
gems I could lap up quietly
feeding my hellfire before
sulphuric emotion could travel from my belly
to my throat and coat every breath.

The ritual of rending flesh is the price for silence but
how much time do I have before
I've been declawed and there is no more blood?

Detox

Healing is selfish.
I won't apologize for
peeling the brown scabs off.
Demands made in ruby shapes.
Gibberish, speaking in tongues that indict
Everyone.
I'm leaving out the pieces of me
you were able to mold and
have since grown cold with disuse
I don't need dried Play-Doh
crumbling in primary colors
colors of childhood that
block the vines crawling out of my mouth
greedy shoots of green that
take what they need.

57% Cacao

My relationship with my mother
is dark chocolate.
When i was younger, it gagged me
overwhelming
rich and bitter
too much for a young tongue
As i grew older, i began to crave
the bitterness that cut
the sweetness to fractions
the lingering taste that always
satisfied even when the cacao
still smoldered in my throat

Zenith

I am healing.
The pieces of me
you took advantage of
will be gone, patched
bright blue over black holes.
Will you be around to share the wealth?
To cup your hands and receive the
cold diamonds which bite your palms
drawing blood payments, rectifying my
ledger.
Red into black
Or will you run?
Unable to match what I have become.

Fatalistic
I blame everyone
when I have made a house
in my refuse
and ignore the knocks on the garbage-clogged door
when told to leave it behind.

My therapist told me
You've got a victim mindset.
What she left unsaid was that
the loophole of perpetual victimhood
is that I am always blameless
my baggage carried by others.
I can never be selfish, or heartless,
or wrong.
How can you ask me to leave that behind?

The Foundation
When the words on my
lips are always *tiredsadangry*
and no one can take the burden
from me.
They become my magic
because I am not here
unless they are.
I am not here by *gracelovemercy*
I have not built my life
on that white sand.

My life has been cemented by mud,
tin cans, and grease.
My house is rage.
I will not knock it down
even when all the occupants have fled
and the fire is rising to the roof.
I only have what I have built with these
exhausted hands
and I will let my creation consume me
if that is all I have.

Beast

My grandmother came from Guadalajara
but the only Guadalajara I know
is down the block on the corner
and smells of burned frying oil.

I am scared to go there alone
because I don't know Spanish.
My mongrel tongue and fickle ears
have always
rejected what it knew I would
never fully be.

Silver Emotion

I'm angry today, tomorrow, and yesterday.
It leaks outside.

It doesn't look like it should.
It is a shining rainbow, sickly gleaming
blue, silver, white
resisting destruction.

Oil floating on water or
mercury in my hand.
I poke it apart
It comes back together
Warmly, chemically, familiar

Rise, foolish woman!

who the fuck are you calling a woman?

I am a sphinx
golden dangerous
slinking through your wetdreams

I am a fist
clenching hard at your throat
bleeding and bruised.

I am quicksand
Inconspicuous, sensuously
pulling you closer

I am.
I am not.
I am undefinable to you,
To them.

To myself.

Where is this?
I scared myself
briefly this afternoon.
Looking at an abandoned scrap of paper,
I found the words
don't get lost
carefully inscribed in the corner
surrounded by pale blue lines on white.

When had I been so untethered that I
had to remind myself to
stay found?

Where am I now?

Am I still there?

Have I made a nest in my lost?

If so, will I recognize the finding or will
it be hastily blown away?
Another note,
on another piece of mind,
something only found if
I am lucky.

Weighted

My eyes are heavy,
the sclera pierced with miniscule hooks
on which other lives softly hang.
My own hook
sways emptily, rattling softly from the gust of
secondhand wind.

Why I Don't Know Spanish
My father drew
a picture of an apple on
an index card and said
Manzana.
My five year-old mouth tasted
the Word, rolled it around,
a feathered lozenge, spat it
out. Mangled, missing a layer.
I mumbled **Manzana.**
No. Manzana.
Manzana.
*No. Listen to me when
I say it* and his voice
clipped the wings of the
new word and then there
were no more
Birds.

Trans-Lite

What do you feel like always?
What do you feel like now?
What about when you wear that dress?
When your hair looks like this?
When we're fucking and your sweet, sweet pussy is riding my dick?

Do you feel like a woman?
Do you feel like a man?

I feel like nothing, babe.
I don't know. I don't really think about it.

How do I say that it's air. Weightless,
necessary to define because it's how
I understand I am alive
but so easy to forget
in the curls and bends of me.
Something I only think of when it is
taken away from me
something I only think about when I am
labelled without my consent.

It's voltage when he says
You look like you're a woman today
because I don't need to be reminded
that my air
is still laced with poison.

Echoes

To repeat writers
before me,
writing saved my life.
Three years went by
a drought

until the psych ward.

While there, I wrote in my head,
forcing my hand into the shape
of a pen
transcribed the walls until
the invisible words
crowded me out of the cell
into the grey morning.

Now, I retch words out,
sticking my finger down my
throat to pull them out.
The words crawl out of the
putrescence
staining the pages
with their vomit-caked curves.

They are still mine.
They shake themselves off.
They seem happier now,
caught by the sun.

I owed them that.

Everything Moves Too Fast
The sky darkens too quickly each day
Time does not stop for me.

My words are magic
binding time to the page.
I make time wait for me
briefly holding it in my grip
leaving imprints of my fingers.

Time is strong and I can only
capture a few moments but
I have grown stronger.
I will make time fear me.

Earl Grey

I'm stuck on the words today.
I feel good.

My language is steeped in
melancholy
A tea bag dropping in boiling water
flavor and fragrance swirling
slowly diffusing in the heat.
When the water is cold, the tea bag
stowed in the cupboard,
I doodle, write lyrics in the margins
content to revel in a loosened chest, air-filled lungs
I'm afraid to make this permanent
I don't recognize myself
without the creeping, weighted shadows

But fuck
Today I'm happy.

Coming Out

It shouldn't be a surprise
that I'm queer
and if it is, well,
I've hid it well for thirteen years,
forced amnesia for most of it,
buried myself miles under
dirt, maggots, skulls.
I would've continued if I had not realized
I am killing myself.

Your local fat Hispanic queer femme
who wants to tear it all down
and remake it in their image.

I'd rather garner tears and prayers
from the ignoble
than
nails in my coffin.

Reflection

My face is my culture
A mirror—of landscapes
that were (are) colonized
broken brown bones
dripping spittle from their curses,
scorching whitehot death.

My face is war-torn, invisibly bleeding
whiteness a thin skirmish over
what they try to kill.
My face pays testimony to
the shattered reconciliation
with our grave diggers
who piss on us before we are even
in the ground

I walk carefully among my people
knowing the white knife residing in my cells
can easily slice them open anew.

Epilogue
I left my mother's house
because the debris from
the years-long nuclear war
was still radioactive
even after all was decimated.

We were still picking up the pieces and I never liked cleaning
up after myself.

Sewing
I used to be a pincushion
needles pushed into my center
and taken out again.
Needles were forgotten, left to gather rust.
I'm too full now.
Shiny, pointed silver fills me.
There is nothing else here.

Missing You

There are times when mania is missed.
Dust piles on shelves, books stay closed, words unwritten, my body is enveloped in a protective stench, hair, teeth, nails unkempt. I am exhausted, and I wish the mania was here with me.
when I'm teetering on the paper-thin edge of control, my eyebrows stay plucked and swollen red, my nails clipped to the bed, I shower four times a day, twelve books lay face-down unfinished and words fill every blank space on the page until it bleeds *blueredblack* and I dance every night on a stretch of cracked, grass-ridden pavement, my heart beating beating beating.

Hurt me more. step back and I'll set myself on fire.
What will be birthed from my flames?
New languages, crackling and sulphuric
I'll reach new heights by pulling myself up with a noose.

Black Cloak
I hadn't really wanted to die;
to die means that you understand finality.
I wanted to show the spikes that had replaced my anatomy.
Death doesn't exist.
Not when the immortality of golden youth resides in my half-shut eyes.

Valhalla

I've made a funeral pyre of canvas and
silver scraps of forgiveness.

One day, I'll finish killing the demons.
On that morning, I'll launch the raft out to
the fickle sea, let flames lick and climb
their way up the mast, devouring each knot.

I will keep watch from the shore until dusk,
turning away when the moon emerges.

Music

I listen to Paquita De La Barrio
and sing along in the heat of the night
stumbling over her lyrics,
swaying on the loose gravel underfoot,
my hands running up and down my sticky hips,
the hills and dips of sensuality that
is free of any gaze
but my own.

I may not speak the language of her tongue
but I flower the same,
twin blossoms of craving and sorrow.

Insectile

I feel myself rustling underneath this old husk.
Reading the lines on my palms creates deeper fissures
ocean-colored and restlessly moving.
What once was small, grew
changed and shaped itself until
it forced integration and I left my old home.

How many small things lie in wait?
How many crusts must I shed to finally
reach the golden-hued center?
When will the royal sun set on this trail of paper-thin exoskeletons?

Day of the Dead
I walk among the sugar skulls
deliciously bright colors fill the tables
jostling with platters of the dead's favorite foods and
old pictures nestled in the vestiges of Catholic afterlife
elaborate altar confections, freshly decorated with love
deathlossgrief are richly pigmented beads strewn across Jesus at
Calvary
This is a celebration and who are we to mourn
when the dead are rejoicing tonight.

Loud Mariachi, cold Coronita with lime, Frida's smoldering visage
at odds with the Virgin's beauteous piety.
I find the courage to go on for another year
Even if I am interrupted
this is my stopping point.

Not Like Eliot's Wasteland
I was trying to find myself through other frames
I forgot where I put my original body.

I created waxwork forms.
Degraded replicas that melted, running through my hands
I could never get close.

I searched and found broken souls that I
soldered back together.
When they were whole, they left me.

I pasted different parts to myself:
papers from unfinished books
batteries from forgotten toys
earrings without pairs
chairs without legs
The paste dried, crusted over
a fragile chrysalis.
Nothing stayed bound to me.

I grew tired of the wasteland
tired of creating from garbage.
I stayed unleashed.
I will find myself
in the ethereal mist ahead.

Anxiety
Each thought is thrown against
the bone of my skull

<u>over and over and over.</u>

Each facet split into hairline fractures.
The thoughts harden
protective of their false brilliance.
Rhinestones that slice like diamonds.
They leave pockmarks, craters in the bone.
Sleep is relief
The dents fill in, the thoughts become feathers
there is peace for five or six hours.

It's Too Loud
On the worst nights
the psych ward isn't so far removed
the mania catches up and
I am waiting for my meds or snack time or
the daily outdoor walk because
institutionalization is
quiet.

Boundaries
I want to say no
without waiting
for the cocked fist.

Moments
Speeding along the dark freeway
no cars ahead
no red lights stopping us
drunk as the fools that
we are.
Music rattles through our bones
shatters what little sense we have left
as we scream the lyrics.
We don't really know if we'll make it
home or anywhere else
before this song ends.
We won't worry about what's next.
Nothing is next when we are caught in
a single drop of reckless.

Wind

I walked along the road
this afternoon.
The Santa Ana's
the smell of fire
on the air.

The plastic bag, double-knotted,
hung from hand,
the weight leaving
grooves in my palm.
I was alone, my phone
silent and I walked along
while the sun set and wind moaned.

These moments of calculated loneliness
are when I feel most
myself.

The irony of not knowing who I am
is that when I no longer feel
the need to define myself, to say
I am "this"
to watch them consume with greedy avarice.

It is easier to
walk down a cracked road,
nebulously
loosely,
an abstract against the sky.

Flaws

I lie
A tick, a quirk, protective coloration
a talent of survival
Pity, deflection, embarrassment,
inadequacy, manipulation, guilt
I've lied for it all.

There is no metaphor, simile.
analogy to make this
prettier
to make myself look
better.

I wrote this down because I'm tired of
keeping track of the lies
I've told.
Maybe they'll hear my words
be decimated by the honesty
recalled to their origins.

If I could take back a
lie that I've repeated in the
thousands
it is
"I forgive you"

Spring
I am flowers
perpetually in bloom
collapse,
or the perfect moment in between.

New Wave Cholitas

Our sad girl image
contrived and constructed
hiding the pain that
leaves our pores
and cuts our lovers to shreds.

Our soul bond,
our founding principle
is a gift,
a safe space,
a love that is
the last refuge when everything
feels dead.

When our backs are against the wall
we meet in the middle again.

Hypromellose
Everything is encapsulated
swirling chemicals, coated and solidified in gel.
Feelings replaced by unpronounceable names,
foreign compounds that
break down in the body or
break the body down.
I wash the pills down with
diet coke, coffee, beer, piss-warm water.
A cacophony of Easter-colored capsules disappears
down my throat
I start another day.

Years
My mother used to tell me,
"Don't shave your legs above the knee,
only prostitutes do that."
In the shower later, I shaved furiously
hoping I would be unburdened
of my sexuality,
a rotted, bloated corpse of desire.
My pastor told me,
"You can't have crushes on other girls,
We aren't born like that."
Days later, I typed and re-typed
"Lesbian sex" into the search engine
preparing the necessary prayers of repentance.
My father told me
my sister told me
my friends told me
and I told myself.
Fear grew from my fingertips
and still does.

Unbalanced
The mug is balanced on an open, upside-down library book
propped on my pillow, on our bed.
The tea sloshes to the edge every few moments,
the liquid jostling noisily with each typed word.
Anthropomorphic animals play golf around the edges of the mug,
rejoicing in early retirement.
Why does our roommate have a cup about retirement,
when every morning she bitches about her waitressing job,
at one of the many burger joints down the street?
Is it a thrift store reject? Purchased for fifty cents,
an attempt to fill the gaping cabinets in the apartment?
Or is it something special, a prized heirloom,
an inheritance molded in white porcelain?
Does it matter?
I have no mug of my own.
I have nothing to fill the holes, no inheritance to bring.
I'd like to break this mug.
But then I would have nothing.

Waiting and watching
Even though I know the cost of remaining still
and the spiral closet that grows closer and darker
and the grooves which I have carved with dragging feet bear witness to
inevitability
I huddle deeper
into the costly blackness, I wait and watch
among the skulls of cowards,
and fall into a small death.

Identity

Why don't you write more about yourself?
He asks.
The problem is these labels
i have stuck randomly on my skin
don't mean shit
if i don't know how i am painted
in every kind of light.

Still

I scoff at the idea that i am creating art
because who the fuck creates anything worthwhile
when sitting in the EBT office at 10 am on a Friday
wishing they had charged their phone last night
and hoping the men sitting behind aren't laughing at
the struggle to hit save

While on break at work
Is it always this hard?
i write it 100 times
exorcising hunched shoulders
and soft words.

Love Letter

San Bernardino
San Ber-nar-di-no
a name that does not trip lightly
off tongues, does not
drip off the lips of luscious women like
honey.

the 909

gang colors burn bright in the white sun
trap music and mariachi blare
from tinted car windows
vagrants line sidewalks, fill parks, wander in parking lots
sex rings in decrepit motels
drug money fill the pockmarks
boarded storefronts, empty houses
police lights flash, glinting on brown skin

bent dandelions
(which are only a weed by virtue of ignorance)

Ode to our ghetto
let us bring our scarred hands
together, ignoring the scent
of gunpowder and blood as we pray
to the patron saints
bless the liquor stores, deliver us from gentrification
guide and guard us from swine in blue uniform
protect this callused skin
because no one else will.

After the initial buzz of alcohol
i don't even need to love
myself
i just want to stop the
Loathing.

My first
tattoos hurt like /blank/.
Insert the thing that cut deepest in the last day or so
finish my simile because
the needles are biting into the soft skin of my thighs
sweat is dripping
I can't hear myself over the sound of permanence.

Fuckability

When I was younger
I used to fantasize being raped
being taken against my will
seen as desirable.
Unable to distinguish passion
from malice.

Even as a child
I was obsessed with desirability
my worth based on whether men
would want me.
Strutting around older men,
waiting to see if they would
turn their heads to look back at me.
Ten years old, begging to be
Sexy.

It followed me
a recessive illness that seeped into
every relationship I had with a man.
The boyfriend I had briefly in
high school and the three boys
I briefly cared about
in college.

When the boy who loved me in middle school
told me that after arguing on the phone with me
he had
wanting to die,
I shrugged.
That wasn't what I wanted.
Anyways, he wasn't real to me.

It still feels like settling
knowing I am loved
without that hint of obsession.

SMALL NIGHTS GOSPEL by gsoell

Never a Beatrice
Or Lolita
The finality of reality steeped
in the knowledge that I am
Ordinary.

Queen Mab

There is a hill behind my college
we used to run
during cross country practice
in high school.
I was never a good runner
always the last or second to last
always too aware of the pain in my body.
My sinews and bones on the verge
of collapse.

As I ran up this steep hill
in the summer heat
sweating, darkness at the edge of my vision
I recognized the hill
from my reoccurring nightmares,
This hill suddenly as familiar as
my fears, an evil place
that sickened me
and I walked the rest of the way up.

Once I was on pills that
gave me dreams so vivid
I'm still not sure if
I had sex with my best friend
or if my heart was broken by the sky.

My sister has dreams so complex
she spends afternoons weaving them
for me, as we drink coffee, comparing
dreams
reading them like palms.

I spend my waking hours
half-asleep, dreaming
hoping that one day
that sickly déjà vu will come again

SMALL NIGHTS GOSPEL by gsoell

and instead of a hill
it'll be a plain with a bright blue sky
overhead, with birds singing gently, with
soft grass and instead of climbing
up up up
and falling
I will be able to lay in the
blue-green grass
peace wrapping me up
like a body bag.

Misandry

I knew I wasn't a woman
in fifth grade.

My choreography teacher
had tight, perfumed jeans and
long teased hair that
warranted third and fourth glances
her figure promising disintegration.

I knew whatever ruinous quality
lay in her, in womanhood
whatever led men to rocks covered by sea
was not in me.

I knew I wasn't a woman
but I spent years looking for the
anything that could
ruin men.

My parents taught me
the shape of mourning
fits perfectly inside love.
Mourning is not reserved for physical death
because the fickleness of life
holds many little deaths.
Choices letter the edges of mourning
twins to the hieroglyphs
within love.
I am sorry,
loverfriendsfamily,
But I cannot fill that empty flask with
what I have learned.

I am sorry
that my love is hollow.

Twins
I've been homesick for you
since we were separated.
Oneness shattered
at birth.

Red Balloon
My life has been a birthday party
where I am an ungrateful child
crying
tears snaking down
my cake-smeared mouth
hiccupping with sobs.
Who wants a bigger cake
expensive presents
hundreds of balloons filled with helium.
Just
more.

Hex
You'll never have anyone else like me
Arrogance dripping off my
forked tongue.
The words clang
metallic and vacant.
Clumsily seamed, belying
a curious amalgam.
I don't have to believe if
you stay magicked
floating in the great buttery clouds of
Illusion.

SMALL NIGHTS GOSPEL by gsoell

our matching tattoos, buffalo wings, that hood store down the street, the color red
I make lists of things I'll miss
when you leave me
So I can love them
Now.

Stop.
You ask me to change
water into blood,
forgetting the miraculous.
Invisible birds fill my feet
eating me from the bottom
up.

Pinocchio
I'm tired of making rules
for myself.
All I want are your strings.
It's easier than admitting
I have no control
of the fishing line that
runs through my limbs
into strange hands.

Self-Care
Every day I write
a list titled
"Why Am I Angry Today?"
The poison seeps into the paper.
I set it aflame, relishing
the crackle.

I Wrote This On A Brown Paper Bag
My life is described in the
refuse of transience.
I write on the blank spaces of newspapers
With stranger's ink
borrowing other lives
leaping out of each
before the end.
Is it possible to learn stillness?
To learn joy in
sameness?

Courage
Is it an unused apparatus
or
is it an apparition
always keeping its distance?

Excerpts

I was swaddled in
porcelain supremacy
fed from milky breasts
worshipped a white man
that was never white
At all.

I grew up telling other kids
"I am half Mexican and Puerto Rican"
as if that changed the
sweet sixteen into a quince the
holy bible into La Santa Biblia.

If language is identity,
what does it mean to
have been shaped by the language
that kills my people
that kills half of me
everyday.
What does it mean to
not know my other
language?
My other language;
a secret that waits for me to find it.

Listening to the chambers of my heart
I wear my hoops
dedicate my life to Frida
listen to paquita and vicente
remake my image into
what I should've been.

You look *whitegrecianjewish*
as if saying I look Mexican would mar
the whiteness of my skin
as if to associate me with

what you assholes think of
as dirt
would be unthinkable
but it exists in my eyes
my hips
my nose
it stays in my heart
bragging "you are, you are, you are"

Are you proud of being white?
No.
Why should I be?
When half of me is descended
from meaning makers, creators
while the other half is
thieves
carrion personified
No.

I saw
an article
asking people to stop drinking
Corona and Modelo
because the company was stealing
water from Mexicali farms
so colonizers could
fetishize the erotic
while drinking cheap beer
the same way they drink
the richness of
nonwhite women as
they fuck them
trying to gain points for
the diversity of their dick
or pussy
game.

SMALL NIGHTS GOSPEL by gsoell

The only thing I am proud of
is that, when he first saw me,
my future lover knew what I was.
A first in 24 years.
noble blood
spilling rich brown.

Guillotine
I cried
because no one loves me.
I can't love myself.

I find a way to blame
the knife trick
(the one that cuts everything away)
On Some/one Else.

Whispers of
"Well, remember that time"
conjuring unmemories
and the *judgejuryexecutioner*
applaud, unchecked
by responsibility.

At Last
Flowers will bloom from
my half-buried skull.
Something beautiful will come
from my rot.
But not today.

Solder
I want to be
transcendent
without the iron-wrought
Wings.

November 5th, 2017
At some point
I'll tell you the truth
about the psych ward.

Yellowing
I am waiting for
the graveyard air to
diminish me.
I am waiting.

Crone
The desert found
my words
creeping slowly, taking my language
even the few words of Spanish:
adios mi amors
bruja, manzana, pendejo, chisme

They snap
dead tree
branches
that are close
to catching
fire from stray embers
that come from
the traitor sun
the sad moon.

Don't Worry, Be
happy
feels like one more thing on my
to do list
than something I actually
want.

Licorice Noose
I strangle my own greatness
before it can
draw complex patterns
from smoke
practice its princely tread.
I kill it before it kills
me
(saving this cursed corporeal form
that loves sadness).

As I Lay In Bed with My Lover
The different textures of
You
make my home.

Softly curling beard is different than
the small coils escaping from your locs.
The velvet on your chest
is respite from the coarse hair
on the curve of your ass.
An alphabet of differences
I've memorized with my grasping fingers.

blind passion

I know the different skins
that make you Whole.
The cool, satin back
warm, pliable chest
supple babyskin of
your face
And the delicate foreskin
I hold in my hands
or my mouth.

These skins wrap themselves
around me
and we share them together.
Lately, they wrap around anything else
and I whisper the fresh laundryscent memories to myself
as I fall asleep.

It All Comes Together

Last night I played with my lover's locs
wove scarves in and out
of his pieces and let them hold him together

And found the text messages I knew
I would find and cried again.
It started the way it always does
But ended differently between us.

But I feel the same.
Outside the sounds are sad,
the crickets are coming inside.
Walls are blurring,
I am blurring too.

Tonight
My words are
suckerpunches.
I pull back before they land
this time.

I choose to blacken one eye
instead of two.
That is my *I love you*
tonight.

Old Hurt in the Bed
In the early morning,
Maybe one or three,
I woke up to the ugly yellow overhead light blaring in my eyes,
While you sat hunched and typed on your laptop
or your phone
It was too early to tell.

Audioslave poured from the television's speaker
I swam through the notes and chords and melancholy
to sit up.

I should've been annoyed,
Should've snapped
Dude what the fuck I have to get up in the morning why are you always playing these fucking games with the lights and music in the goddamn morning and why this song when this song makes me sad because it reminds me of us but not the us from the karaoke night when you first came home but the us when we were sitting at the bar in the middle of the afternoon and I was too afraid to tell you that I loved you because you were leaving and I didn't want you to feel bad so please stop playing that song tonight I am unraveled come to bed.

Instead, I kissed your shoulder and said
I love this song
and went back to bed.

Melting Honey

When I'm on top of you and
I slip you inside of me
your hands clench my hips so hard
I have bruises the next day.
Words lose meaning.

Fucking isn't the word for when we clasp hands
gently kiss *shouldersnecksthighs*
murmur "I love you baby."

Having sex is too clinical.
It misses the sensuality
our grasping hands and lingering tongues.

Making love is some corny white people shit.
It forgets the scratches
the question "whose pussy is this?"
the screams and slaps.

Words have failed me.
I cannot succinctly define the breathlessness
that fits together to complete something that
goes beyond us
into divinity.

Why Do I Scare You?
I could be your everything your best friend your love your rock
he types to other women, swearing it isn't what I think.

I've been here longer
and you still haven't given me your worst.
How long should I wait for your best?
I can believe they're empty words, baby.
Not because you love me.
You just don't know
how to reach the grandiosity of your cons when it comes to
the hard parts of love.

Cracked
You run from this
even though there is nowhere to go
crashing into walls
breaking everything
cracking me open.

Your face is all I see
through the plaster dust and frenzied twirl
of debris
twisted, grimacing
eyes black with panic.

Why?
I whisper.

I don't deserve this. You. Anything.

I walk through the jagged
grasping, slicing pieces
to you.

Steel Spine
In those rare moments I allow myself
to resent you
to feel the hurt and anguish knowing you
looked in my eyes, mouthed
I don't want nobody else
and tried to find someone else anyway,
let other people disrespect me.
I waver between trying to change myself,
my facets that you tolerate
or demanding you appreciate the
love, support, pussy, everything
I bring.

I contemplated leaving you,
letting the last image be your clenched fists and straight back
as you walked away
after staring at me dry-eyed, mouth drawn tight
against your disgust.

There was no miraculous revelation,
no deux ex machina which saved us.
I did it.
my arms, my back, my legs.

You don't see the strength in kissing you, touching you, speaking life
to you
because you don't see the grace, forgiveness, mercy
because you don't see how much you've done.

I still think about you, worried.
How will he feel?
To know that sometimes I'm so fucking angry?
To know the immensity to which he fucked up?
Will he stay?
Would I stay?
Knowing the seeds of resentment bloom

SMALL NIGHTS GOSPEL by gsoell

unexpectedly
always unwelcome.
I don't know.

I refuse to continue to take the burden of blame
the burden of undeveloped hearts on my shoulders
the burden of responsibility for the scars left by other hands.

So I make myself the rook that
clunks on our wooden chess board.
Make myself into a multitude of flickering eyes
that look at
your dethroned king.
Make myself into words
that twist into the shape of a Cheshire
and say:
What next?

Giants
We are two rocks
standing with dignity
in the vivid desert
erosion crumbling our smooth faces
sun bleached smooth
reaching up to the orange sky

turned towards each other, always
watching, watching
in the frosted night

Dinner

It struck me
while washing dishes last night
        warm water sluicing dinner down the drain
        wind rattling the glass in the windowpane
        winter darkness settling in
that if you left
I would still have
        the bowl I stole from my mom's house
        our sex-stained blanket
        three bottles of beer chilling in the refrigerator
        my dog-chewed phone charger
        a mostly finished bottle of argan oil sitting
        in the back of the bathroom drawer.
I'll be damned if that
isn't what makes us
synonymous with freedom.
I don't have to be here.
I don't have to be anywhere
I don't want to be.

Your Phone

When I hear you typing all I can think of are the times I went through your phone and read the words that you typed to other women words that belonged to me before you forgot why you decided to be here in this hot little room why did you tell them I was jealous and controlling why did you tell them I was a shadow in your life why did you tell them they mattered if you hold me every night like I'm your tether to this earth to your sanity and I whisper **I love you** and you scream it back and all our words the thousands of words we typed and spoke are underneath us and they weigh us down but I suppose, at this point, they weigh me down and you are floating.

baby, you look so good up there, with the bright, bright sun and I can't stop staring as you fly higher and higher into the blue sky.

Away.

Punch-Drunk
You orgasm like you are drowning
Gasping for air, clawing at my skin
Like my pussy is the only
thing you've ever known.

Inhale
Exhale

You grab your phone off our nightstand.

I don't exist
the rest of the night.

Substitute Teacher

The one sweet moment
happens at 3:30 each school day.
The autumnal weather
seems to frame the
look of relief on the
faces of each father as they see
their children
who shriek
"Daddy!" and run
Home.

It reminds me of you
How happy you'll be when you have
the chance to do better than your father.

Trust Me

What's funny is that I did.
You underestimate how much
my senses were honed by
shitty men.

The scent of rot
isn't difficult to find.
Like cigarette smoke,
it ground itself into my clothes
stained your hands yellow.
Made our room fog with
disease.

Moonlight reveals all in
the witching hour.
I didn't sleep for 29 days
decoding the faint hieroglyphs
on your back
until I knew all.

I open the window.
Scrub your back until the fresh,
raw skin appears.
I try.

Temporarily
The scratches on my back are healing.
It seems too much to ask that
you re-open what you left to heal.

Tornado
You were not ready for me.
Another promise
that proved impossible to keep.

Waves

My archetype for love was a marriage built on
black, slick stalagmites that curved steeply
into the ocean.
How fitting I should seek out the same cliff face
to jump off every night hand in hand with you.
Yet,
you helped me fit constellations inside myself
gave me words to the starlight shining from my eyes.
It's betrayal to write one without the other
to memorialize the hurt
leaving the candied love behind.
Allowing our worst to be
immortalized and
what we leave behind when we become one with the sea.

Bully

It's laughable to realize
I hold the power to hurt
as much as you do.
I've spent so much time wielding it
double-edged and heavy.
Unconscious and asleep.
I wonder why I wake with aching arms and tired back.
Why you are lying in a pool of your own blood
dying?

Erosion
Everything about us is hard
because we are hard people
wrapped in layers of lust and rage and regret.
Layers that slowly melt as soft water
runs down
over and over.

SMALL NIGHTS GOSPEL by gsoell

Is This How You Love?
I didn't feel inadequate until
you introduced "I Wish You Were"
to me.
Who smiled at you
the way you liked
new
still shining for you.

Who had long hair
that longed for the tangle of your fingers
Hair that didn't refuse your words
whose black eyes promised
what I never did:
total absolution for every sin you would commit against them.

Whose body you didn't know,
a well that had not gone dry.
Uncomplicated newness that didn't lie
next to you every night and
beg for your love.

Whose heart remained shut
bared to you
granite that you could not find a
fissure with which to burrow your way into.
A heart that didn't care about you.

I was never equal
I even failed at turning myself hard
staying softly open
my heart:
useless flesh, blood, ventricles and blue veins pulsing softly
cavernous
allowed you to fold into the space you left.

I've lost my voice to a cold this week.

SMALL NIGHTS GOSPEL by gsoell

My heart aches this week because I am sick.
Last time I was sick
my mind unhinged for a month
you left.
I can't help but think
it's only a matter of time before
the tissues piling up on the nightstand
the cough drop wrappers littering the bed
the perpetually filled mug with chamomile tea
will conjure up
"I wish you were" again.

Cyclical
I like that you challenge me
even when it hurts like hell
shifts my perspective
makes a liar and hypocrite of me.
Do it again.

Bitter
If love is said
without the weight of the grindstone
then it is a:
Tin painted gold, rhinestone encrusted,
made in China, found at the swap-meet, cheap motherfucker
that will stain your wrists green
every time you wear it.

Pavlovian
I lay in bed
legs spread
masturbating to the thought of you
touching other women the way you touch me.
Breaking the circle of red thread
armoring against possibilities
shivering into reality as I come back to you.

SMALL NIGHTS GOSPEL by gsoell

Argument
We are dust mites caught in the sun.
It feels so hot and narrow
when we bind twin hatreds together.

To my Rivera
I want to write letters to you
like frida did diego
and when we are dead
they will read my words
weeping, beating their fists on the floor
as passion flows painfully to their chests
even in the great blackness
our shared madness
fractures into rich colors
let the hurts be legends
our movements cast in bronze
our faces turned toward the other.

Weekend

I said we were
pieces of the same puzzle
the first time we tried to make love
while our bodies were frozen
crystallized by fear.
I said we were destined
that we fit together seamlessly
because our legs tangled in motel sheets
was what they meant when they defined
infinity.
I said we were one
while there were only twelve hours
before we changed our shapes back to
what they were before.

My Love
I create worlds
oceans
plains
mountains
deserts
as I weave language.
But I can't create stability
from nothing at all.

Golden One
You've flown too close to the sun and
I'm no good with charred
wings that are not mine.

The Origins of Thursday
The sound of us
sleeping
is thunderous and violent.

Motherfu-
I want to scream
HOW MANY MORE TIMES
into the void
that is curiously occupying space
near my frontal lobe.

In the semidarkness,
my perpetual twilight,
this yawning vacuum
sneers at Pandora and
locks *griefjoyangerhope*
inside itself
leaving
exhaustion
and nothing more.

Fill in the Blank
I've crossed everything
out except
587 lines that whisper
*"I just don't want to feel sad about you
anymore."*

A God, Magic and A Psych Ward

Every day you were gone, I lit a blunt
a flame offering for my god—
a god of rage and impulse,
constantly rearranging and shaping himself
into glorious pain;
I would offer a blood sacrifice but
this opened wrist offers no reprieve
dust pours from my torn throat
and my heart pumps uselessly;
I have nothing but my infinitesimal magic

Day 1

      I watched everything from my hazy cocoon
      saw myself
      become the person you've always wanted
      fun.
      Interesting.
      Someone who lived loudly.
      My phone buzzed over and over
      and I tried to frantically shove notifications into
      the leaking, noxious, weakly-pulsating sack of heart—
      It didn't work.
      I make dates that I pretend to keep
      knowing this is the band-aid over the wound that reads
            "Your lips look so soft."
            "I heard your best pictures are R-rated."
            "I want to suck your beautiful nipples."
      Smoke pours out of my nostrils;
            God. I want to forget.
                Please.
                Please.
                Oh God, Please

SMALL NIGHTS GOSPEL by gsoell

<u>Night (An Interlude)</u>
My talent, my magic
is pushing you away.
with each word,
I weave ropes around your waist
make it hard for you to
run
but hard for you to
stay.

My household god
that I shut in my ribcage
and let sing beauty
that only I can hear
that only I can worship.

Suffocating my need
knowing the song grows muffled
and the wheezing between words
grows more frequent.
Still I am incorrigible.

Does intent matter if you are not the one who is stuck?

<u>Day 2</u>
I woke up without the usual battle
and didn't have to shove you or turn away
or suffer silently as you settle onto my side of the bed—
I was alone.
I light up again, in gratitude.
Our bed couldn't hold both of us
and our sadness.

I would've been pushed out,
my body and mind permanently stretched
and bent out of shape;

no longer in need of comfort or softness.
At least, that's the decision that was made.
Your pain takes over our bed.
At night
your body burns hot with it.

5 a.m.
I wake up—
freezing
and I missed you.
Even your pain, your sleeping selfishness, your fire
is velvet night for me.

Night (A Distraction)
How did we get here?
>Backwards, I mean.
>A place where I feigned disinterest
>and distance.
>Quiet wars in my mind
>"But what if…"
>"He'll leave you and…"
>"Why the fuck would you…"
>And I am exhausted.
>And I understand why you are too.

It's the sharp silence that draws blood.
>Dull half-understood
>anxieties are passed out like candy.
>You take them home to your heart
>and allow them to scrape you with
>each movement
>until the red scraps
>curl around your ankles.

I sheath myself, hoping hoping hoping that
>it's enough.

SMALL NIGHTS GOSPEL by gsoell

Stop, I whisper desperately
at my heart-stained hands.
Just stop.

Day 3
I woke up with Dread.
The same one with a different face attached
I take a hit
and then another.
No sacrifice for you today, lover.
Dread gobbles it, greedily, *sloppily*

The sticky chunks fall from its mouth
and I am powerless to stop it.
Or am I?
That's what I say on the bad days.

But when every day is a bad day
and my chest has a vice grip on my lungs
and my mind vacillates wildly like a child on
a swing
and Dread is the one staring at you,
the one holding a pillow to your face,
where is your reprieve?

And where is mine?

Noon (An Invasion)
Cried for the first time since you left
    50 hours
        old mascara tumbled down
        I turned my phone off.
        So what if you come back
        if only half of you returns.
                    if only a quarter of me returns.

SMALL NIGHTS GOSPEL by gsoell

Night (An Omission)
How funny that
after all the apps and messages
and men telling me I'm
Something
I wanted
needed
had to hear
that I wasn't as poisonous
as I thought.
I didn't get that.
I'm what I feared.

Day 4
I didn't know we were dying
and the moon is full tonight without you.

There were things you lost in the fire
and things I'm losing as I flick this lighter on.

I'm not sure what you lost
but maybe I should've
been the lost thing.

Day 5
I have nothing for you
again.
Not by choice
but everything I had yesterday
is behind a locked door in the ward.
I have what I left behind:
My body, papered in blue scrubs
and yellow socks with rubber grips

and a thin white blanket to keep in my small warmth.
My mind is locked away too.
A block of ice is here.
Reflecting the cold around me.

"Dumb bitch"
The words are hurled like a phlegmy expulsion
from a smoker's throat
yellow, stinking, viscous
and they slide down my throat
and I laugh hysterically.
Only your truths hurt.
Visiting hours are being alone
but with uncomfortable jokes and
resentment wrapping my heart further in
the ashy remnants of before.
The ice retains nothing.

I am not here.

<u>Day 6</u>
How do you tell someone that the broken coins
you've given them
can eventually be redeemed
and dropped into a slot
clink, clink, clink
and a plastic egg with a new
You
will drop into their hands
warm, fresh, and soft.

How do you tell them the long walks
and long hours of sleep
and the silence
will eventually end.

SMALL NIGHTS GOSPEL by gsoell

How do you promise a future that
remains uncertain
and unformed
because you have been carrying that
picture with you for years
and it's creased folds and
dog-eared corners
mock you.

How do you warn them
it would be easier
to find another?

<u>Night (A Revelation)</u>
They type *cannabis abuse*
as if I was not merely replicating
the haze I lived in
with you.

I have only the sharpness of my anxieties
but no sharp objects
to let them out
I rub a wrist frantically
on the smooth plastic of the nightstand
and the bed.

And contemplate the simplicity
of being trapped with these thoughts
in a room that is never dark.
Where there are specters outside the
perpetually open door
every 15 minutes.

<u>Day 7</u>
Do you feel hopeless and helpless?

and how can I reply with anything but
Yes.
Actually
I'm mad as hell.

Why can't I get you or them or
every other fucker
out of my head
when I should be the center of my
life?
Why do I spin
balls, chain, whips, collars,
idols, shrines, altars
out of my straw
and where the hell can I
learn to make gold?

When I was a child
I heard sibilant whispers through the wall
"trust me"
"this happened because you didn't trust me"
"you didn't love me enough"
"she gave me the attention I needed"

My mother was a husk
because she didn't trust enough.

and the hollowness has begun in me
My feet ache from the new lightness.

<u>*Day 8*</u>
  "Why are you here?"
  "What triggered the event?"

And I say

SMALL NIGHTS GOSPEL by gsoell

Well, I haven't been sober in a week and my laundry is piling up and my boyfriend left our love to try another and 24 years is too many consecutive years of pain and the check engine light came on in my car, and while looking at that blinking little light, I decided that swallowing my antidepressants with a couple of Bud Lights and finding a really sharp knife may not be the worst thing for me in this moment.

"And do you still feel helpless and hopeless?"
And I think for a minute, feeling the insect probing on my face, half-heartedly trying to reach the brain through my *earsnosethroat* and sigh. I want to go home but my home has been dissolved with our acid more than once. At the very least, I want to be gone.

> **I mean, I guess not.**
> Which is a lie but how can I say,
> *Well, fuck, man, that's just my day to day.*

After (A Prologue)
When you, my household god,
step out of the Uber
and say to the driver,
"Thanks, man."
and pull your suitcase from the trunk
and stare at me
and the hospital bracelet still circling my wrist

All I can think is that

if you died, I would forget your voice,
your face
your hands
but never the exact texture and smell
of the skin behind your right ear.

SMALL NIGHTS GOSPEL by gsoell

SMALL NIGHTS GOSPEL by gsoell

Afterword

It's January 29, 2019. I wrote this collection in November and December of 2017. Things have shifted and I don't think that some of these poems would be the same if I wrote them now. And that's beautiful to me. I never wanted to be stuck. I keep pulling myself out of mud or barbed wire and I'm bleeding and ithurts but I'm moving forward. And that's what I want to end my collection with: forward motion.

Thank you. Thank you. Thank you.

SMALL NIGHTS GOSPEL by gsoell

About the Author
Denice Gsoell is currently a substitute teacher in California. They hold a Master's degree in English Composition from CSU San Bernardino and are interested in social justice in education. When they aren't teaching, they're playing with their dogs, reading, or drinking iced coffee. This is their first poetry collection.

www.ingramcontent.com/pod-product-compliance
Lightning Source LLC
Chambersburg PA
CBHW021409290426
44108CB00010B/454